Text Copyright 2013 by Dianne Shearer and Sarah Grant
Illustration Copyright 2013 by Sarah Grant

All rights reserved. No part of this book may be reproduced in any form or by any electronic or mechanical means, including information storage and retrieval systems, without express written permission from the publisher, except by a reviewer who may quote brief passages in a review.

First Edition
Shearer, Dianna and Grant, Sarah
Nana's Hair
ISBN 978-1484150597
Fiction, Children

Nana's Hair

By Dianne Shearer and Sarah Grant
Illustrated by Sarah Grant

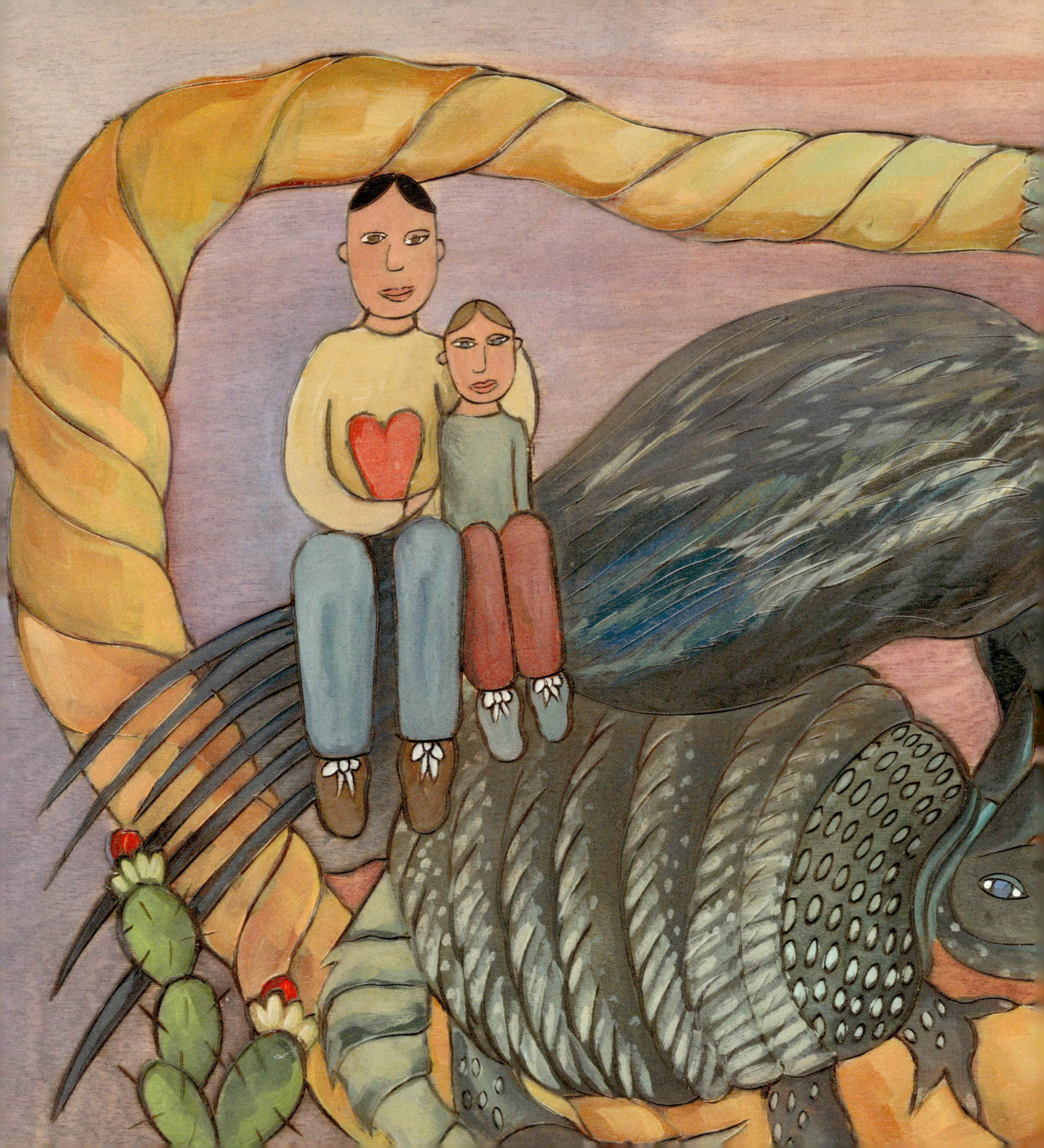

My name is Tyler.
And my little brother's name is Nicholas.

It is my job to help watch out for him.
We live in the desert where rattlesnakes,
armadillos, and roadrunners also live.

Our house is surrounded by prickly cactus and wild flowers.
After the winter rains, springtime arrives.
The cactus and wild flowers come alive.

In the summer and autumn it is very hot and dry and
the blooms are gone when the sun shines brightly in the
great big western sky.

I call my grandma and grandpa Nana and Papa.

They live far away on a lake where there are fish, deer, long-legged blue herons, and many other woodland animals.

Their house is surrounded by tall pine trees, birch trees, lush grasses, and forest wild flowers. After the winter snow and cold comes springtime rains. Leaves bud on the bare trees and wild flowers begin poke their heads out from under the forest floor.

In summer the sun shines and sometimes it rains, so the forest and lake shore are deep green and wild flowers and grasses are in full bloom. By autumn the leaves begin to fall from the trees and the forest prepares itself for winter.

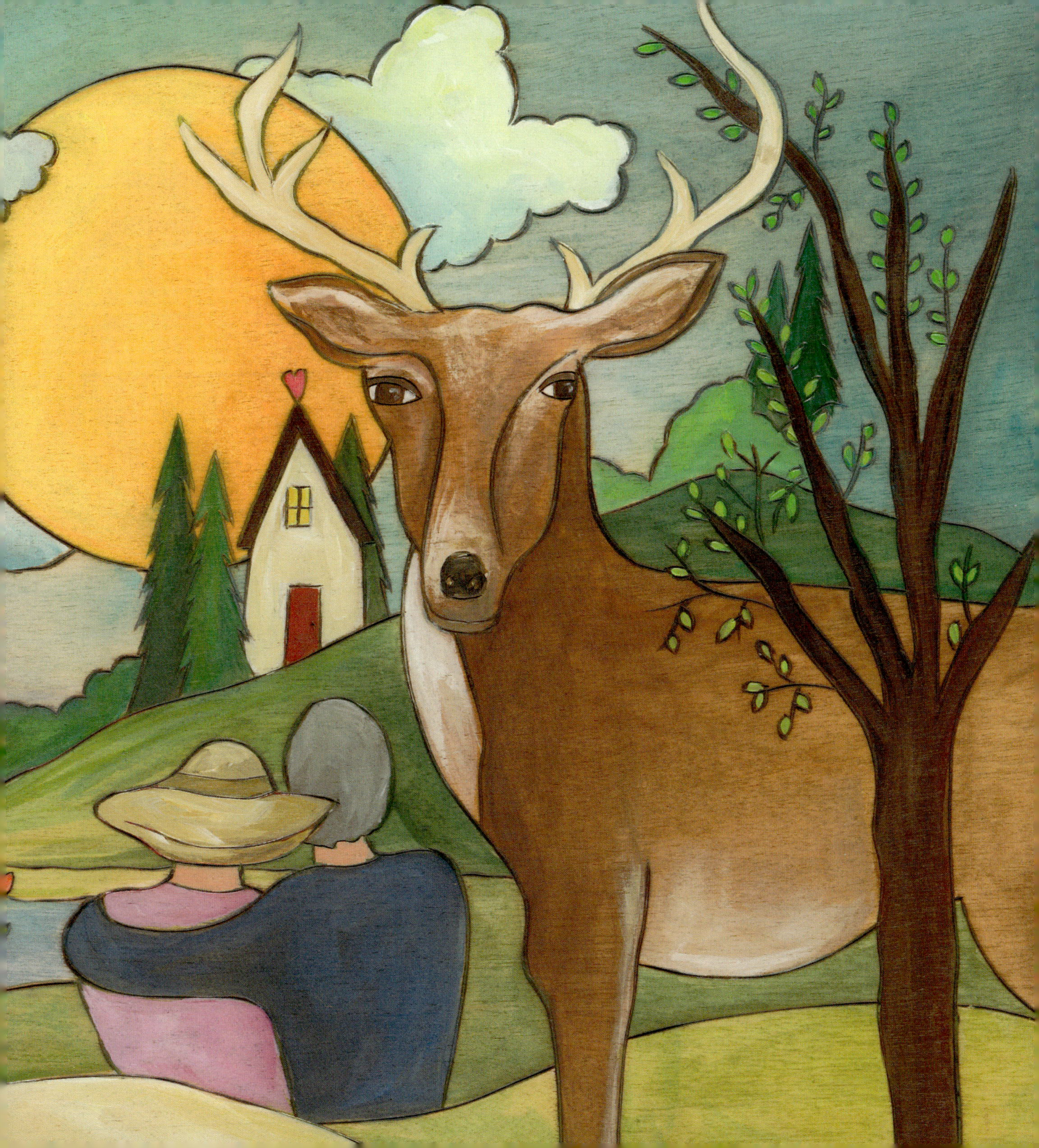

I am Nana and Papa's first grandchild, which is special.

Now they have many more grandchildren, including Nicholas.

Best of all, we have lots of cousins to play with when we visit the lake and the forest.

We swim every day until the sun sets low over the lake.

We have bonfires in a forest clearing and roast marshmallows.

Each night we see the moon rising and the northern sky is filled with a million stars.

I am always excited to go to the lake and visit Nana and Papa and all my cousins.

But this year is different.
This year I am kind of scared to go because my Mom and Dad told me Nana is sick with cancer.

Cancer is a disease.

You need to go to the doctor for special care to get well.

Until I get to the lake,
I am going to dream,
of all the fun things we do with
Nana and Papa.

I am going to think and pray that Nana gets better soon.

On the long car ride to the lake,
while Nicholas was sleeping,
Mom and Dad told me
that Nana needed strong medicine
to get well.

The
medicine
can make her very tired
and
upset her stomach.

I know Nana might not
be able to do all the fun things with us
that we do every summer.

That makes me sad.

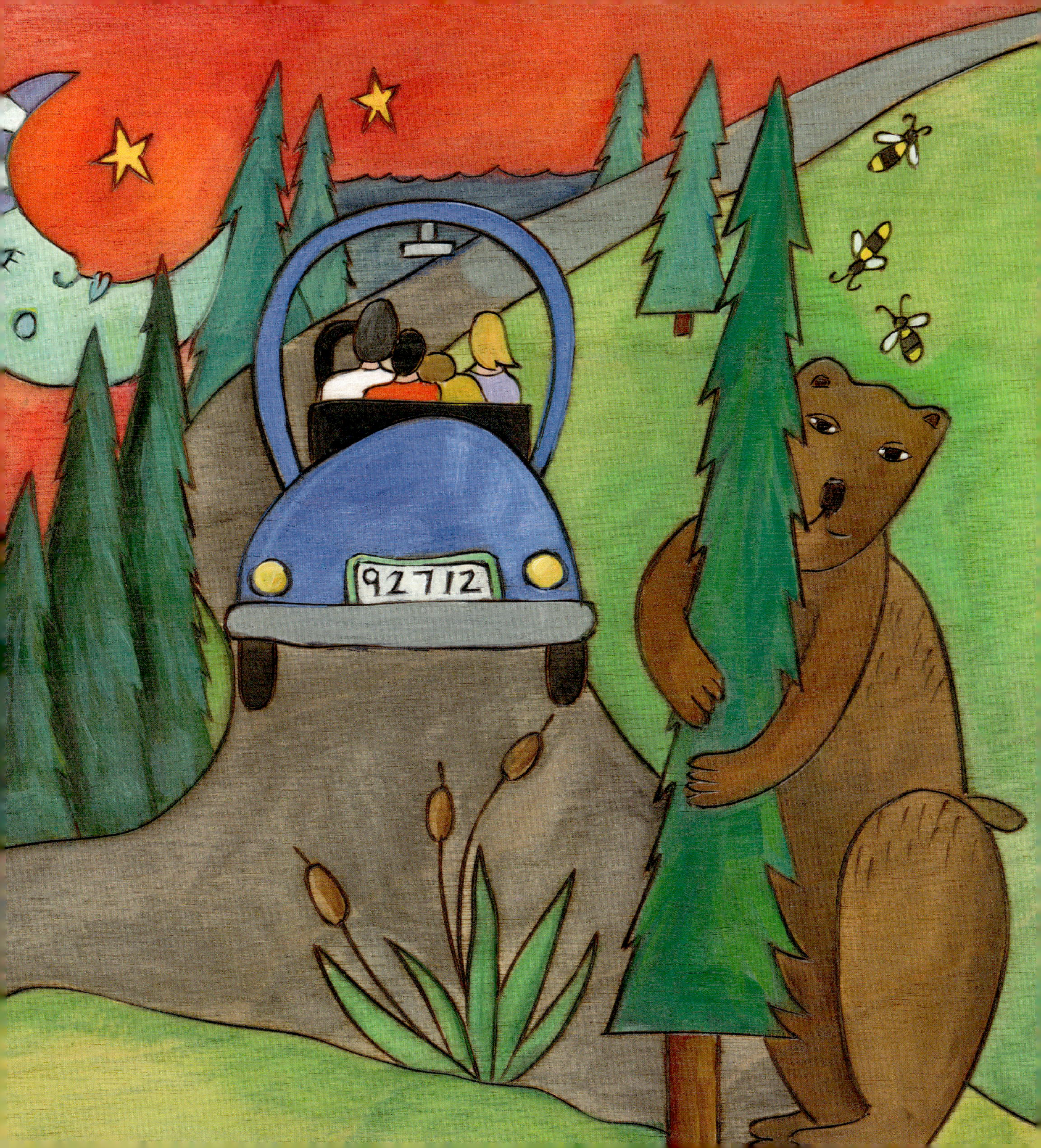
92712

When
we
arrived
at the lake,

Nana and Papa
were there to give us big hugs
and the fun began!

We slept in a tent,
picked wild raspberries,
and had a watermelon hunt in
Nana's garden.

We played fetch with their
dog Barney.

I was so happy
I forgot Nana was sick.

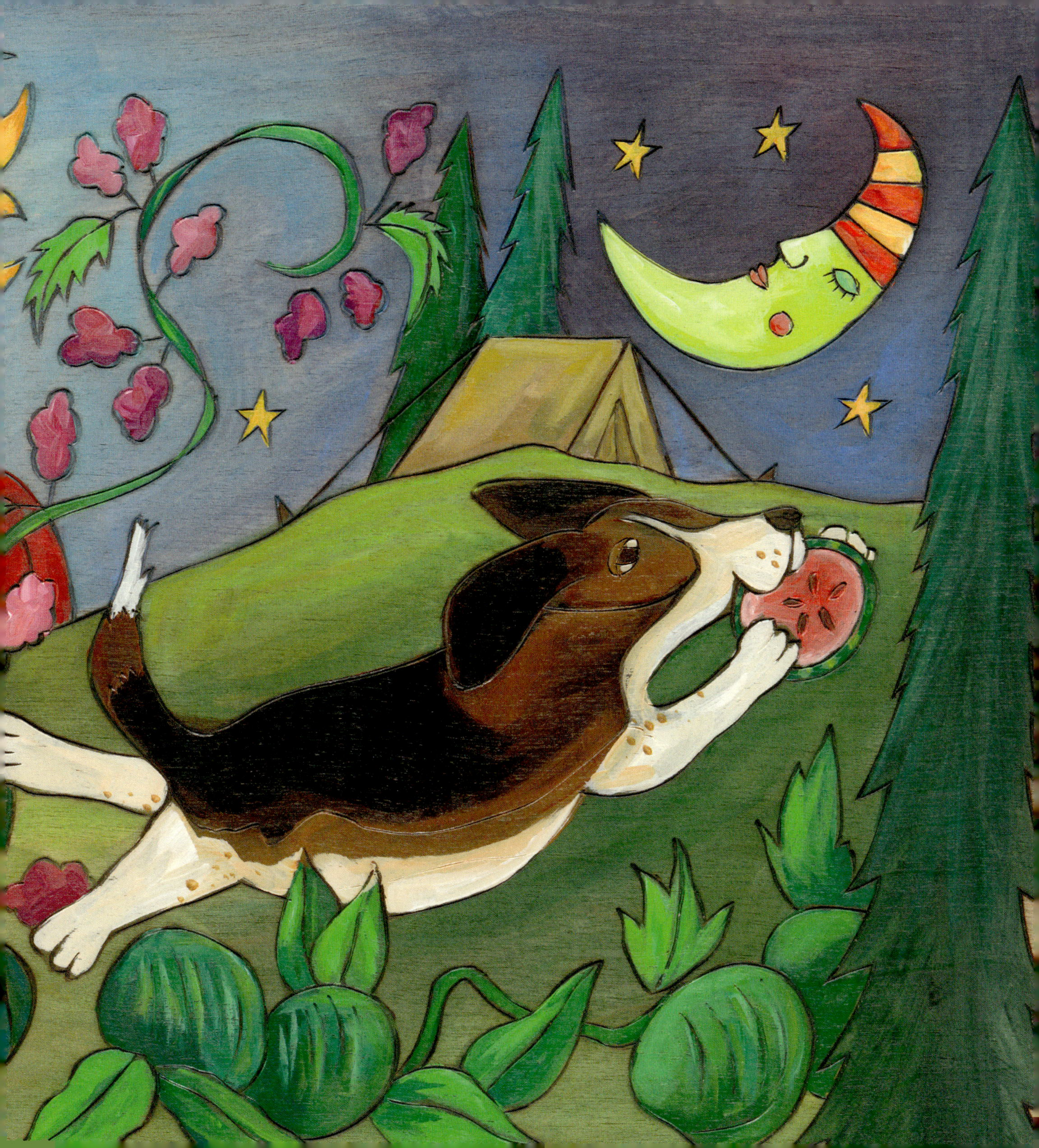

One night at the lake
there was a very big thunderstorm.

I was scared and decided to go sleep with Nana, Papa and Barney. As I tiptoed into their room, Nana heard me and quickly put a pillow over her head.

I thought this was a new game Nana was playing.

Before I could ask about the game Nana asked, "Tyler, can I tell you something?"

I am a good listener, so I sat quietly on the bed and listened.

Nana held the pillow on her head.

She told me the medicine the doctor gave her for the cancer made her hair fall out, but that it also made her well. Nana told me that her hair would grow back so I should not be afraid.

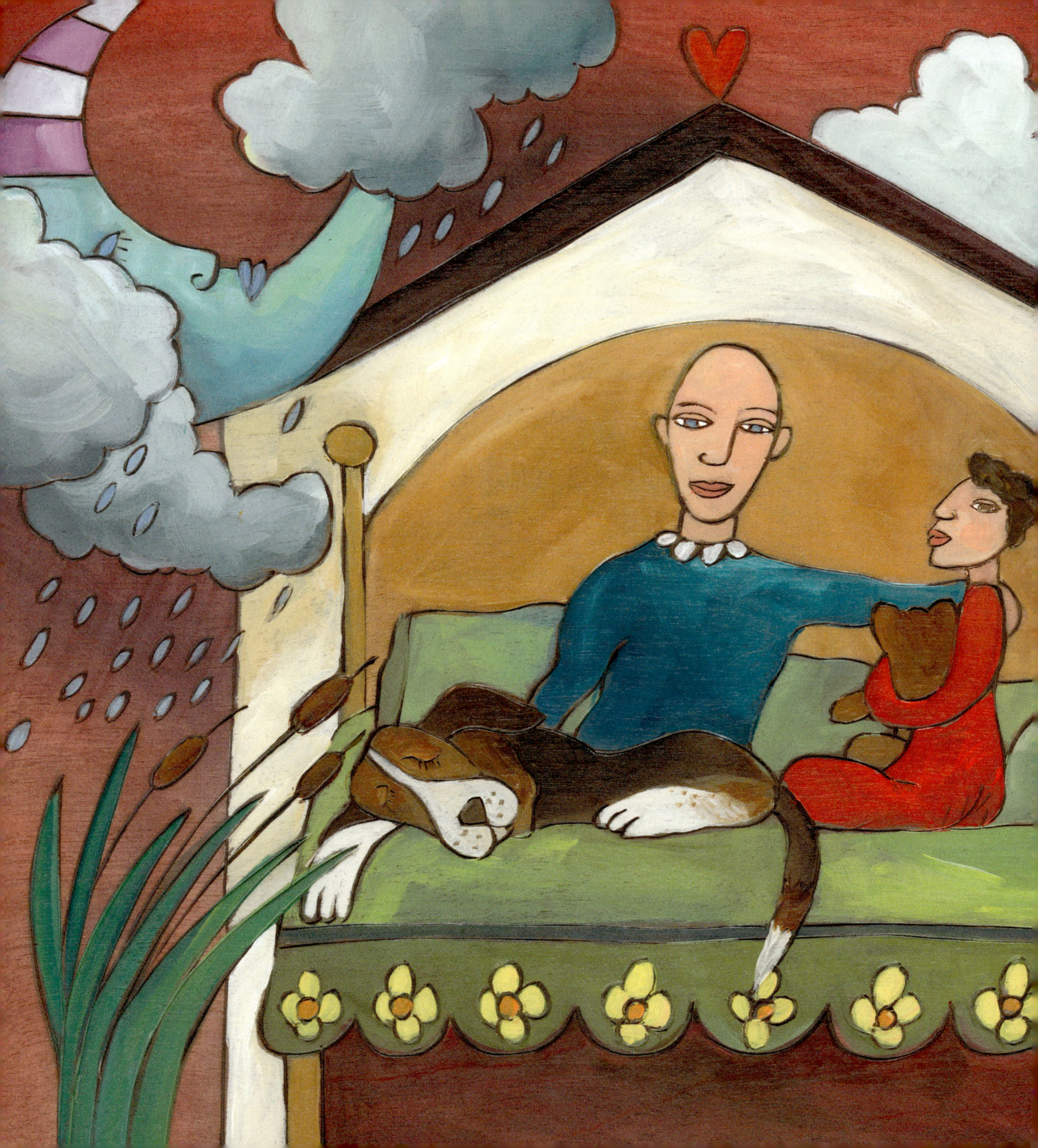

Little by little Nana took the pillow off her head.

She did not have any hair.
At first I was scared.
Nana looked strange to me.

I love my Nana and I got used to her with no hair. I believed what she told me, that her hair would grow back.

Medicine is a good thing, even if it makes us feel bad for awhile.

Nana reminded me that when Barney had to take medicine, it made him tired and he lost weight. Now Barney is plump and frisky just like he used to be because of the medicine.

Nana and I cuddled in the rocking chair by the window.

We watched the big thunderstorm roll over the lake, and I was not scared any more.

She told me she has lots of hats, scarves and wigs to wear until her hair grows back, so the little kids would not be frightened to see that she has no hair. They are too little to understand everything about cancer and strong medicine.

Nana told me she was proud of me for being such a big boy and listening so quietly when she told me about her hair.

As I rocked in her arms I fell asleep and dreamed of all the fun times we would have at the lake for many years to come.

Nicholas and I are a lot older now.

We can fly alone in an airplane to the lake. I am blessed to have Nana and Papa. Nana is healthy and all her hair has grown back.

I still live in the desert with the prickly cactus, wildflowers, rattlesnakes, armadillos, and roadrunners. The sun still shines brightly in the great big western sky.

Nana, Papa, and Barney still live on the lake with all the pine and birch trees, wildflowers, fish, deer, and long-legged blue herons.

The moon still rises in the northern sky.
And there are a million stars to count each night.

Dianne Shearer's Personal Story

Author, Dianne Shearer, lives in Waukee, Iowa with her husband Leon Shearer. After treatment for two different types of cancer, a stem cell transplant and the loss of her hair, Dianne is five years cancer free. In the telling of this true story regarding her hair loss. Dianne wanted to help families understand that the trauma of hair loss due to cancer treatments can be a blessing in disguise. That blessing is a continued "Hope for a Cure", an understanding and compassion for the loved one with cancer, and showing that through the love of family and friends we can all survive trying times. While Dianne's story focuses on two of her grandsons and her cancer and hair loss, she is now the proud Grandmother of 10 grandchildren. Life is good and Dianne's cancer and hair loss are in the past.

Sarah Grant's Personal Story

Sarah is an abstract painter, illustrator, and founder, owner, and lead designer of nationally recognized Sticks Inc. an object art and furniture business. Sarah holds a BFA, MA and MFA all in the Fine Arts from the University of Iowa. She resides in Des Moines, Iowa with her husband and their three dogs. Sarah and her husband Mark are the parents of six children and so far the proud grandparents of two.

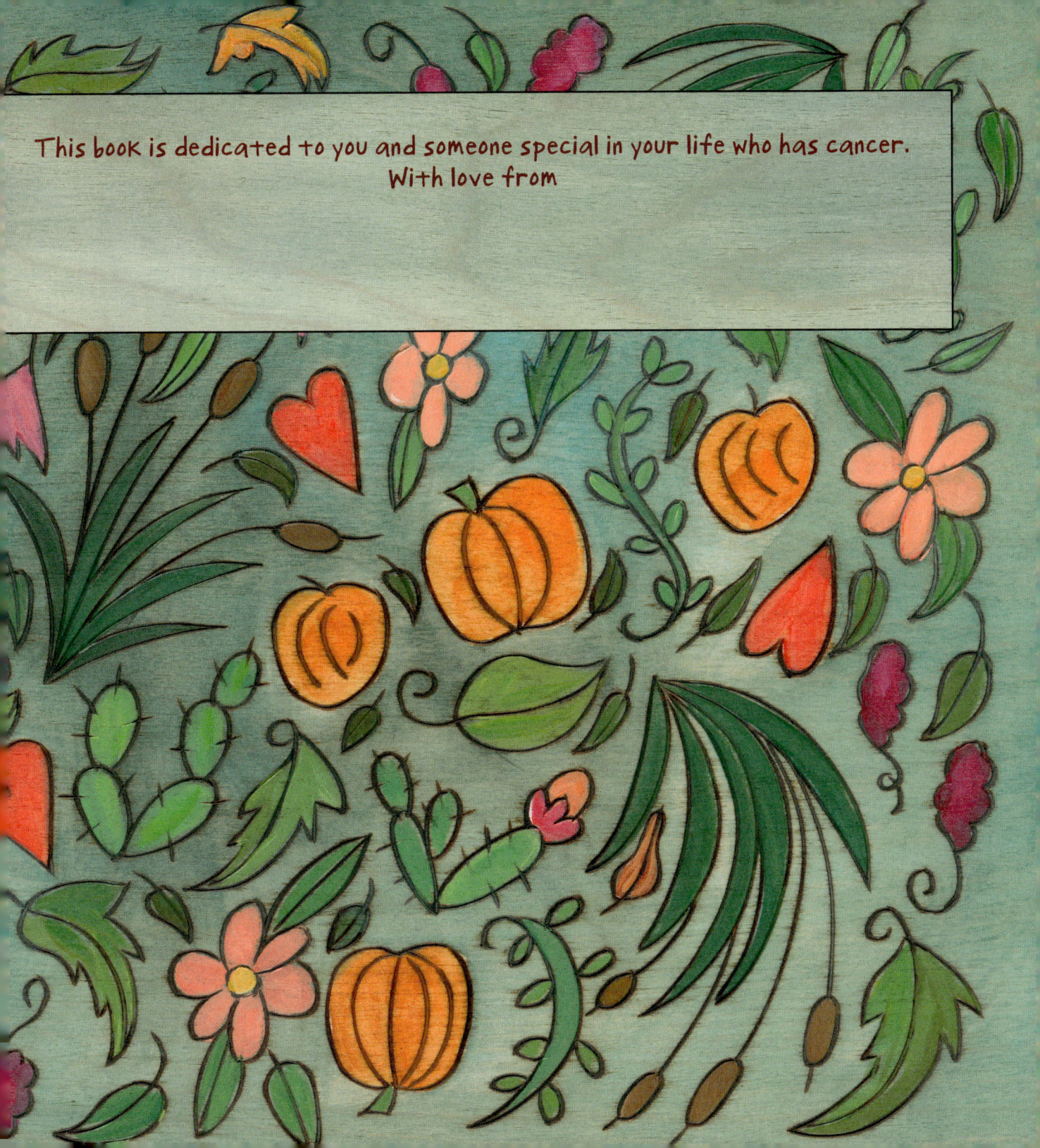

This book is dedicated to you and someone special in your life who has cancer.
With love from